Mildred's Letters

Isabel Reyes

ISBN 979-8-89130-948-7 (paperback)
ISBN 979-8-89130-949-4 (digital)

Christian Faith Publishing
832 Park Avenue
Meadville, PA 16335
www.christianfaithpublishing.com

Printed in the United States of America

Acknowledgment

This book is dedicated to my Lord Jesus Christ and my sister Mildred, who wrote these letters dedicated to our Lord, Christ. God has given me dreams and visions to find letters written by my sister Mildred. I thank the Holy Spirit for leading and guiding me as I write this book.

Thank you, Lord, for your guidance and wisdom to bring light and life to my sister's letters to Jesus Christ.

Contents

Introduction

My sister Mildred wrote letters from God to His earthly friends and also letters from my sister to her beloved Christ. These letters have been hidden for fifty-five years. This is the story of how God has guided me to find letters through dreams and visions. These precious letters were written when Mildred was eleven years old.

May God's guidance and divine directions introduce this book to whomever has ears to hear and an open heart to receive it.

Chapter 1

Our Steps Are Ordered by the Lord

My sister Mildred was my mother's ninth child. She was very funny and witty. She was born with one kidney. I remember most of her childhood life was spent in and out of the doctor's office, having different types of tests done because of her condition. At age sixteen, our family doctor—a very gentle and kind person, that is the way I remember him!—said to my parents that she needed to be transported to a hospital in the United States; her only kidney had stopped functioning. In the mid-'70s, the technology in Puerto Rico was not advanced enough for her to survive the treatments she needed to have. Since the treatments she needed were not available in Puerto Rico at that time, my mother searched for family members living in the United States. My mother had her older son and daughter living in the States.

My mother Julia and sister visited with Jenny, my mother's second child, to see if the Chicago area would be suitable for her and her health needs. As they researched places for her to be able to be treated, they found out Chicago would not be the right place to go for her needs, between extreme weather and resources. "To me, God had different plans." A Bible verse comes to mind!

The heart of man plans his way, but the Lord establishes his steps. (Proverbs 16:9)

God is always working for our good. Most of us are spiritually blind and don't have the relationship with our Lord Jesus Christ for Him to lead us in this, Fallen world. We need His guidance and direction, for us to fulfill the part of our destiny that is not clear to us, but He has Ordained for us to fulfill. After all the searching, my mother and sister ended up going to California. My mother's first-born lived in Orange County, California. Robert was able to help set up a household and found a hospital close to where the family would be settled. The Lord again guided their steps!

This is the hardest part of my sister Mildred's story to tell since all I have seen and remembered was pain and suffering for all involved in her life and care. Mildred endured all her pain and suffering with smiles, and her laughs kept her spirits up! By the time I came to California, my mother, Mildred, and my youngest brother, Rafi, had been living in California for three months. By then, she was established at UCI Medical Center and was getting the treatments she desperately needed. Mildred had surgery to introduce a fistula in one of her arms in order for her to be connected to the dialysis machine, which is the treatments and protocol the doctors used to clean her poisoned blood caused by her kidneys not functioning any longer. There were hope and cries and laughs. This was the beginning of what she endured for eight years.

Chapter 2

The Collision of Emotions

The collision of emotions in all her endurance, trials, suffering, and pain—I knew she had Jesus inside of her. Jesus was guiding her. No one that I have known personally in the past and since then have endured what she went through to stay alive. Her demeanor and the love of God and family are what kept her fighting for her health and well-being. In her prayers and letters, she wrote to Christ as a child; she asked for strength and for Jesus to be with her! "This is what a relationship with Christ is all about, giving your heart to Him and letting Him comfort you." I know in my heart that God collects your tears and your prayers in a bowl and sends His holy angels to protect you and to give you strength when you need it the most! *She knew that at a very young age.* A Bible verse comes to mind!

> Casting all your anxieties [tears, burden] onto
> Him, because He cares for you. (1 Peter 5:7)

I was listening to a Christian podcast yesterday afternoon after writing for a while, and the person on the podcast said, "God sent His only begotten Son to earth to die for us. He was cast out of towns and chased out of cities. He was dragged through the streets. He came to pay for all our sins. God did not spare Jesus from suffering—dying on the cross was the ultimate sacrifice." I said to myself, "How did God the Father endure all that Jesus suffered when He was on the cross, seeing Him stricken and bitten?" A heart-wrenching feeling came over me. How did He feel? Heartbroken? He paid our slate in full. If God the Father didn't spare His only begotten Son, why should we be any different? Why should we be spared from pain and suffering? God the Father did not spare Jesus's life and well-being! I ask myself, Did God the Father feel every heart-wrenching whipping Jesus received? Did God the Father collect every tear and every drop of blood Jesus lost on the way to the cross? How did a sinless Jesus's body end up so corrupted? The Bible gives us glimpses of Jesus's life and death—I hunger to know more, don't you? I may never have all the answers to the questions I'm posing to you. The Lord knows all things, and someday He will reveal secrets to His faithful servants.

> Be joyful in hope, patient in affliction, and faithful in prayer. (Romans 12:12)

To me, Romans 12:12 says it all. *Jesus offered His body as a living sacrifice* to atone for all our sins. It brings comfort and joy that God the Father loves us so! My sister earned her angel's wings and graduated to heaven at age twenty-seven, with many, many trials, surgeries, pain, and suffering. I knew that in heaven there is healing and wholeness.

Her death was very traumatic for my whole family, but at the end, there was comfort in seeing her at last at peace, with her earthly body now resting. *She is with Jesus Christ at last.* Nothing is worse than losing your younger sister, but I knew she was in the best place, and she was comforted by the Most High, her Christ, as she called Him in her letters. After all these years passed, I don't think I had time to mourn her death. I find myself bursting into tears and sorrow every time I sit to write her story. I suppose God has a purpose and a time on how He heals our hearts.

Chapter 3

Quest to Discover Letters

This is where God has guided me through dreams and visions to find the letters Mildred wrote at age eleven. She wrote the letters over a span of a year. Mildred did not write a date on them, but she left clues of the year she wrote them. The first letter she wrote was from Christ to His earthly friends; two other letters were conversations she had with Christ, pleading for grace and strength. My prayer: Lord, help me and guide me. I'm opening some wounds that I thought were healed!

Chapter 4

Letters Written by Mildred

Mildred had a precious childhood photo album with letters and photos of family and friends. She was very protective of it and always kept it close to her heart. After she passed, I have kept her album for thirty-eight years. I have carried it and moved it everywhere we have gone. At times, I have opened it up and looked at the pictures. I don't remember ever reading the letters since I recognized that these letters were precious to her. I was still honoring her by keeping them private. By God's guidance through dreams, now I realize that her letters were to be saved and unveiled in God's timing.

Letters Written by Mildred Specially for You

Friend, it has been a long time. I have been walking alongside you. I follow you wherever you go, but you never noticed me. When you have troubles, I make them my own, guide you, and give you advice and comfort, but you thank others. When you are sad, I see your heartaches, and I mourn with you and comfort you. You don't realize the sum of tears I collect from your cheeks! When you are full of joy, I rejoice with you. I desire that you know that I'm always at your side so your joy might be steadfast. At times you say, "I have no friends," and it grieves me that you have never sought me. I desire to be your friend. I sincerely desire to be your faithful companion. But you have not sought me or recognized my guidance. So this is the way you express yourself!

You say you have never had an opportunity to have a relationship with me. Yes, there are many who talk about me, and the ones who have recognized me rejoice in that moment in my presence, and *I celebrate with them*. They talk about me on the street corners. They talk about me in the schools. They talk about me in the temple. *Behold, nature talks about me*. I want now for you to seek me. Open the doors of your heart and accept me as your *faithful friend*.

Love Christ.

Class-Time Prayer

> Lord, I feel lonely in the classroom; I have no one to talk to. I don't know if I go outside and abandon myself to You, Lord. I need You, Lord. Never forsake me. Lord, give me strength to answer in class so I can make progress all the days of my life. At times I think You have forsaken me, and You don't love me, and the whole world hates me. I can't keep going like this. Lord, give me strength so I don't lose Your tenderness and Your peace. Give me strength to continue participating in class. Give me more strength to keep seeking You.
>
> Your child,
Mildred

As I translate this letter, I remember her struggles with health issues. Mildred was born with one kidney. She spent a lot of time at the doctor's office, so she missed a lot of school classes. She wrestled and pleaded with God to give her strength.

> I lift up my eyes to the mountains—where does my
> help come from? My help comes from the Lord,
> the Maker of heaven and earth. (Psalm 121:1–2)

How many of us struggle with health issues, mountains, and valleys? Have you ever thought to surrender it all to our Lord Jesus Christ—and sit at the feet of the cross and give it all to Him? At the tender age of eleven, my sister did it. This is childlike faith. She knew Jesus Christ was her only help. Where did she get the idea that Jesus is our strength, might I ask? In my heart, the Holy Spirit was guiding her. Sure, we went to church, but the church we went to just performed rituals. We went to the priest to confess our sins. We did not go directly to God. *But my sister did.* Think about what I just said. If our help comes from the Lord, why are we not coming to Him directly and crying to Him so we can hear directly from Him? What a game changer.

> Come to me, all who are weary and burdened,
> and I will give you rest. Take my yoke upon you
> and learn from me, for I am gentle and humble
> in heart, and you will find rest for your souls. For
> my yoke is easy and my burden is light. (Matthew
> 11:28–30 NIV)

Are we listening and understanding what Jesus is telling us? To me, He is revealing and guiding me. This is an invitation to lean on Him only. Do not depend on others and your own understanding. Jesus is the only way.

> Jesus said to him, "I am the way, the truth, and
> the life. No one comes to the Father except
> through me." (John 14:6)

Do you understand now that there is only one way to know and have a relationship with our Father in heaven—through Jesus Christ? I say hallelujah, and thank You, Jesus!

The Hour of Grief

Lord, I find myself alone in my room, a place of refuge. Help me. I feel lonely before You. At times I abandon You. Christ, I desire to be Your apostle. I want more of You. My spiritual body, my soul belongs to You, only You. Give me strength, Lord, so I can go forward. Surrender to me, give me, Your peace and Your tenderness. I ask for more strength, Lord. I surrender it all to You, Lord.

Your child,
Mildred

As I translate my sister's letters and prayers to Jesus, tears flow down my face. It has been thirty-eight years since my sister had passed. God led me to find the album she had kept these prayers in through a dream I had a week ago. I said, "Lord, where are You leading me?" I'm reminded of God's promises. Tears in scripture are meaningful to God, and He collects our tears in a bowl.

John 11:35 (KJB) reads, "Jesus wept." Jesus is a very compassionate person; He is also our Most High God. He hears our cry and comforts us; that is how my sister saw Him. That is why she was always in touch with God's character and sought His face. My heart is full of emotions because I never knew the spiritual side of her. She was eleven to twelve years old when she wrote them, but I know in my heart that the Holy Spirit led her to write these letters and prayers—heartfelt prayers that fill your soul with hope and yearning for more of God's goodness and mercy!

Blessed are you who hunger now, for you shall be filled. Blessed are you who weep now, for you shall laugh. (Luke 6:21 KJB)

Thank You, Lord, for this is a promise that I will treasure all the days of my life.

Chapter 5

My Story and God's Guidance

I'm one of Mildred's older sisters. I was number seven out of thirteen, so I was assigned from a very young age to help with household chores and help take care of the younger siblings. After school, I always helped with washing my youngest brother's cloth diapers and washing dishes after dinner. I didn't mind it; it gave me time to dream. I was babysitting at a very young age, which gave me some responsibilities and accountability. I was in my second year of college in Puerto Rico when I was taken on a trip to California to visit with my mother and sister. I thought it was a vacation, but no! I didn't know that I only had a one-way ticket to California! Again I had to take responsibility and help with the day-to-day responsibilities and make sure my sister had the support she needed. My training has always been a part of the family support system—for my mother and especially my sister.

Always caring for others. Many of you might relate to that, especially if you were part of a big family. A support system is a big help, especially for your parents, knowing that they can count on you to help whenever the need arises (believe me, with my sister's health and needs, there was always a need for support). I want to take a minute here and thank God for the strength and a willing spirit He has bestowed upon me; that is the only way I could have made it through all the years of trials and tribulations! So I left my studies and college behind.

Coming to the USA was a complete *culture shock*. I had to go to school to learn and understand the language so I could be prepared for whatever life throws at me.

Always willing to learn and help. God was taking me through a life process—*destiny*. God always puts you through a learning process, even though we as humans only see the present circumstances. We don't see the future as God does. He knows what is in store for us.

Chapter 6

Dreams and Visions Are Bridges to Your Destiny

Two days ago, I said, "I'm stuck, Lord!" His faithfulness always comes through. He spoke through my dreams again and said, "Dreams and visions are bridges to your destiny." I'm in awe of His guidance and faithfulness! He reminded me that I had some more writing to do; He brought up Natacha as a reference. *Natacha* was the name of a telenovela we as children used to watch. This was a story of a poor lady who used to work as a maid for a very rich family. She was put through trials and tribulations as a result of her falling in love with the son of this rich family. That is how God guided me to find my sister's letters through speaking and referencing "Natacha."

My sister Mildred kept newspaper clippings of the telenovelas that were popular when she was writing the letters—clues I have used to date the letters. She wrote the first letter in 1968 (Mildred was eleven years old then). God knows all things, and He speaks to you in your own language and life experiences. God even gave me the song that they used to play at the beginning of each episode. It goes like this: "The past is gone, a new bright day is dawning. Oh, Natacha. Oh, Natacha." I have not heard or remembered that song since I was fourteen years old. Isn't God amazing? I'm in awe of His guidance and the grace He has given me to be able to write about my sister and her precious letters.

In the last days, I will pour out My Spirit on all
people. Your sons and daughters will prophesy,
your young men will see visions, your old men
will dream dreams. (Acts 2:17)

Pay attention to your dreams and visions. His promises are His
guidance to your destiny. Dreams and visions are open windows
from heaven!

Chapter 7

God's Guidance to Find Mildred's Letters

How God Guided Me to Find Letters That
Have Been Hidden for Fifty-Five Years

> For God may speak in one way, or in another, yet
> man does not perceive it. In a dream, in a vision
> of the night, when deep sleep falls upon men,
> while slumbering on their beds, then He opens
> the ears of men. (Job 33:14–16)

Through my dreams, somehow I knew I was supposed to write a book! In November 2019, the week that would have been my sister's sixty-second birthday, I received a dream. I was given the colors of the book cover and the title for the book. I saw a book with a blue-and-yellow cover, and I heard God say, *Your book to write*. I remembered half of the dream and wrote down what I remembered. I had forgotten half of the dream and the title of it! So I wrote a prayer for God to remind me of the rest of my dream!

In January 2022, I was reminded again in a dream that I needed to look at my sister's photo and letters album (part of the dream from November 2019 that I had forgotten). I got up with the intention of

14

looking for my sister's precious album. My dog needed to go out, so I forgot to write down the dream and forgot to look for the album. My dream was blocked again.

I have looked at the album from time to time but never read the letters. I respected her privacy, as I said before, and the album was very dear to her! Again, God gave me another dream on February 8, 2022. This time He referenced "Natacha" in my dream and guided me to look for Mildred's album. That is when I read the letter Mildred wrote to her beloved Jesus Christ. I broke down, and tears rolled down onto the letter as I was reading it. A collision of emotions came over me as I read the first letter and then the second. My heart was, at that time, in pieces. I said, "Lord, forgive me for not finding these letters sooner. Do You think these letters were hidden for such a time as this?" God's timing is always perfect! Here is Mildred's original handwritten letters to her beloved Christ! The first letter Mildred wrote is from Christ to His earthly friends. The other two letters were from Mildred to her beloved Christ.

My prayer for all people who pick up this book to read: May God give you dreams and visions. May God open your eyes so you can see His guidance clearly. May God give you clear direction for your new journey with Him. May God bless you!

Chapter 8

Mildred's Handwritten Original Letters

Especialmente para ti

Amigo

Hace tiempo que camino contigo.
Te sigo donde quieras, y tú me lo notas.
Cuando tiene un problema lo hago mío y
te ayudo, pero otro le das las gracias; si estás
triste al verte así me entristezco y te consuelo,
pero tú ni te fijas en la cantidad de lágrimas
que recojo en tus mejillas, cuando estás alegre me
alegro contigo, y quisiera que tú supieras que yo estoy
a tu lado para que tu alegría perdura.

A veces dice: — "No tengo ni un amigo",
y me duele al saber que nunca me has buscado
a mí, que yo si quiero ser tu amigo, fiel
y sincero compañero, pero no has buscado ni
conocido, así te apreso.

¿Qué nunca has tenido oportunidad de
conocerme? Pero sí muchos por los que hablan
de mí, y los que me han conocido, únicamente si
recoges al leer en algún momento, mucho me
alegra al estar con ellos. En la esquina habl.
de mí en la escuela habla de mí en los templos
hablan de mí y en la misma naturaleza... Contempla
Habla de mí.

¿Quisieras ahora encontrarte conmigo,
abrirme las puertas de tu corazón y aceptarme
como tu amigo

Amor
Cristo

La hora de la tristeza:

"Señor" me encuentro
sola en mi Cuarto y
lugar de refugio, Ayúdame
me siento sola a ti, Pero
a veces te Abandono, Cristo
quiero ser un Apóstol
más de tu iglesia; un
Cuerpo vacío si no Con
alma para ti, tuya Señor.
Dame fuerzas señor
para todos seguir
Adelante, dame la Resignación
la paz, la ternura y más
aún Dame Valentía Señor;
Valentía siempre. Para seguir
Contigo.

<u>La hora de clase</u>:

"Señor" me encuentro sola en el salón de clase no encuentro con quien hablar, no es a salga a fuera pero me siento sola y te abandono Señor: pero más te necesito Señor en clase no me dejes Nunca. dame fuerza para Contestar en clase para poder seguir Adelante toda la Vida, A veces pienso que tu me Abandonas y no me quieres y que toda el mundo me odia.

No puedo Señor seguir Asi toda la vida Señor, dame fuerza para no Perderte y dame la ternura la Paz pero más Valentia para seguir Contestando en clase no puedo más. dame Valentia siempre para seguir Contigo.

About the Author

Isabel Reyes had been a nurse for thirty-five years. After Isabel retired, God guided her to be ordained in the healing ministry. That is when Isabel started having more visions, dreams, and additional guidance from God.

Isabel and her husband, Larry, live in Southern California with their two Yorkshire terriers, Nate and Zoey, praying for people for their healing. Isabel enjoys cooking, gardening, and taking walks with her two Yorkies.